First published 1983 by Editions Gallimard
First published 1984 in Great Britain by Moonlight Publishing Ltd,
36 Stratford Road, London W8
Illustrations © 1983 by Editions Gallimard
English text © 1984 by Moonlight Publishing Ltd
This revised edition © 1990 by Moonlight Publishing Ltd

Printed in Italy by La Editoriale Libraria
ISBN 1 85103 093 X

THE BOOK OF
INVENTIONS
AND DISCOVERIES

DISCOVERERS

by
Jean-Louis Besson

translated by David McAree

MOONLIGHT PUBLISHING

for Pascale

On 24 November 1974 archaeologists in Ethiopia dug up the remains of a 20-year-old girl. They called her Lucy. She had lived there about three million years before.

Lucy was small and slightly stooped; she belonged to a hunting and gathering community. She and her people probably already used crude stone tools.

Two million years later in Java, *Homo pithecanthropus* is rooting through the undergrowth with sticks in search of vegetables and small animals. He sleeps in caves and is able to 'borrow' fire from natural bush-fires. This keeps him warm as well as frightening off wild animals.

Homo sapiens, our great-great-grandfather discovers how to make **fire** for himself about **80,000 years ago** by rubbing sticks or flints together.

The two-sided flint. A sharp, multi-purpose tool is made by carefully paring both sides of a piece of flint.

80,000 years ago

40,000 BC   By standing on **floating tree-trunks** men can transport timber and can travel easily.

Wooden-frame shelter.
Easy to put up and covered with skins, this early tent can be carried by nomadic hunters.

Hot soup. Containers made of skins would burn if hung over a fire, so the cook adds red-hot stones directly to the soup.

Pebble and bone **jewellery.**

30,000 BC The first ever **painting** is done in vegetable dyes and earth on cave walls. It may be that writing too began from pictures like these.

25,000 BC **Specialized tools:** a stone axe, a bone knife, a fish-bone needle.

10,000 BC Its intelligence, its sense of smell and its need for company have made **the dog** man's best friend, at home or out hunting, for 12,000 years.

7500 BC **Lake villages** built on stilts to protect men from enemies and wild beasts.

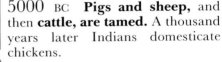

5000 BC **Pigs and sheep,** and then **cattle, are tamed.** A thousand years later Indians domesticate chickens.

Weaving. Wool is woven first, by the Egyptians. Then, two thousand years later, linen and cotton from India are woven.

Canoes made from animal skins stretched tight over a reed frame and caulked with pitch against leaks.

4000 BC **Pottery** appears in China and around the Mediterranean.

3000 BC **The wheel.** This is the first *real invention*, because it was not copied from nature: it was not inspired by feet, wings or fins. It appears first in the Sumerian City of Ur (in modern Iraq), the birthplace of Abraham.

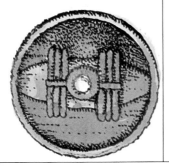

One of the earliest pictures of a wheel indicates that it was made from three pieces of wood strapped together. It probably rotated on a fixed axle.

9

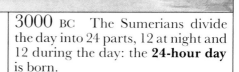

3000 BC The Sumerians divide the day into 24 parts, 12 at night and 12 during the day: the **24-hour day** is born.

2780 BC Egyptian priests calculate the **365-day calendar.**

2500 BC **Gold ornaments, metal mirrors, linen clothes, wigs, board-games, tables, stools, beds, tweezers** and **combs** are common in Ancient Egyptian households.

The **safety pin,** and **glassware,** in Egypt.

2500 BC   Known to the Chinese and Persians 2,000 years earlier, the **plough** is now in use all around the Mediterranean.

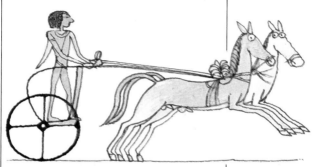

Horses pull **chariots** with spoked wheels.

In Northern Europe the Frisians get around on **skis** and **ice-skates.**

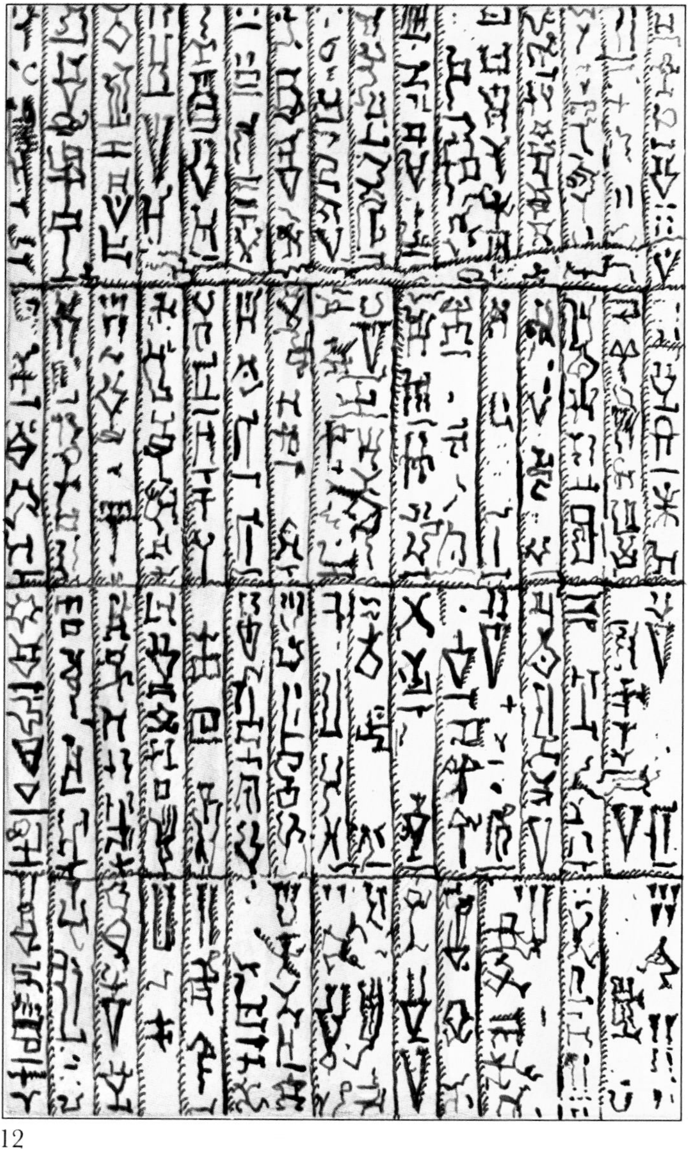

The first **writing** - cuneiform - appears around 4000 BC in Mesopotamia (now Iraq). It consists of little, wedge-shaped patterns scratched on clay tablets and is used more for book-keeping than for story-telling.

Some years later, the Egyptians invent a new system of writing, by symbolic pictures; we call them hieroglyphs.

Writing can now record all human knowledge, from medicine and mathematics to the lives of the pharaohs engraved on the coffins and found in the pyramids. As only a few people are literate, the writing is done by a small group of professional writers, the scribes.

As writing develops, so do the skills of making ink, brushes and paper. The Egyptians write on papyrus made from the bark of a plant growing on the banks of the River Nile.

4000 BC

13

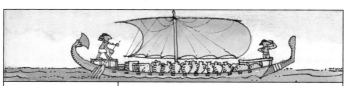

2000 BC The wooden-hulled **merchant-ship** has a square sail and a steering oar. In these boats the Phoenicians (from present-day Lebanon) can sail several days at a stretch out of sight of land.

1500 BC The Egyptians tame **the cat** which they worship and even mummify after death. A thousand years later, cats are introduced to the Romans who so far have used stone-martens to chase mice. In the Middle Ages every European house has a cat, to kill the black rats brought back by Crusaders.

A B

1000 BC **The alphabet** is first invented by the Phoenicians and then adopted by the Greeks. It is called after the first two Greek letters: *alpha, beta*.

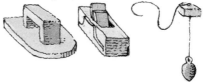

800 BC The **plane,** the **trowel,** the **saw** and the **plumb-line.**

776 BC Dedicated to Olympian Zeus, the first **Olympic Games** last five days. Subsequently they are held every four years, with a gap from AD 394 to 1896. Greek girls and boys are passionately fond of sports.

690 BC Gyges, King of Lydia (in modern-day Turkey) strikes the earliest **coins** ever found.

600 BC **Electricity.** The Greek mathematician Thales notices that if he rubs amber it attracts dust. He assumes the existence of a fluid which he calls *'elektron'*, Greek for 'amber'.

500 BC The Romans have **oil lamps, tiled roofs, broad cloth** and **paved streets and roads.**

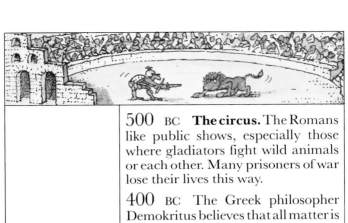

500 BC **The circus.** The Romans like public shows, especially those where gladiators fight wild animals or each other. Many prisoners of war lose their lives this way.

400 BC The Greek philosopher Demokritus believes that all matter is composed of the identical minute particles that he calls **atoms.**

300 BC **The sundial.**

The Greeks invent the **water-clock,** which can be used to measure, among other things, the length of a politician's speech.

The saddle. For horseback riding.

300 BC **Aqueducts.** With their building skills and their knowledge of hydraulics, the Romans bring **running water** and **drains** to their **bathhouses** and villas.

The four-horsed **Roman chariot.**

250 BC Archimedes designs the **solar mirror** and, of course, the **Archimedes screw.**

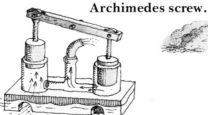

150 BC Ctesibios invents the **suction pump.**

280 BC The **lighthouse at Alexandria.** Built of white marble and lit by a wood fire, it is one of the Seven Wonders of the World.

120 BC **Barrels, beer** and **long trousers** in Ancient Britain.

AD 80 Hero of Alexandria invents the **first steam engine,** the **aeolipyle.** It will have to wait until the 18th century to be properly developed and put to good use.

Soap, wooden chests, jam in Europe. **Chess** in India.

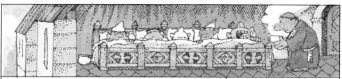

AD 368 Christian monks found the first **hospitals,** meant to isolate lepers as much as to cure the sick.

Slate roofs and **tiled floors** are used in building houses in Europe.

AD 500 The **triangular sail.**

AD 800 French children begin going to **school.**

AD 800 **The horse collar.** Bearing the weight on its shoulders, one horse can now pull a heavier load than four horses could before, with their harness across their chests.

AD 900 **Shoes** for horses and **stirrups** for horsemen.

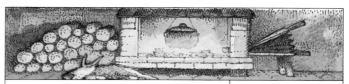

The **fireplace.** By now, most houses have proper stone fireplaces, replacing simple hearths and smoke holes in the roof.

AD 1000-1450

Windmills and **watermills** have already been in use a long time in Persia and China.

Around AD 1000 they are introduced to Europe. Little by little their mechanical power takes over much of the work done until then by the sheer muscle-power of animals and men.

Windmills grind corn and pump water to drain marshland.

For more than 700 years watermills are used to power factories: sawmills, forges, tanneries, paper mills and even mints are run on water power.

Tallow candles of mutton fat or lard might smell awful, but they are much cheaper than those made of beeswax.

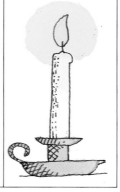

Around 1100

UT queant laxis
REsonare fibris
MIra gestorum
FAmuli tuorum
SOLve polluti
LAbii rearum
Sancte Iohannes

Cathedrals are built with the help of wheelbarrows, hoists and winches. Stained-glass windows allow in the daylight.

A Benedictine monk, Guido d'Arezzo, invents the **tonic solfa** using the first syllable of each line of a Latin hymn. **Do** and **ti** are to come later, as will the fixed musical scale, ABCDEFG.

1190   The **magnetic compass** reaches Europe, although the Chinese have used it for years.

The **goose-quill pen.**

1 2 3 4 5 6 7 8 9 0

1240   **Arab numerals** replace Roman figures.

1250   People begin to take baths — occasionally — in **tubs.**

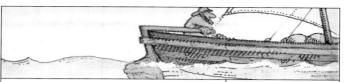

The **stern rudder** makes steering a boat easier and replaces the two oars used up to then. It will take another 200 years before it is in general use.

Hourglasses and **eggtimers** for measuring time.

1300 Edward I is presented with a **fork** and thinks it is a new sort of weapon. Its use will not become common for another 250 years.

Scissors.

Buttons for clothes.

The **mechanical pendulum clock** replaces the water clock. Pope Sylvester II is said to have designed the clock in the 10th century.

1350

The earliest-known picture of anyone wearing glasses is an Italian portrait dated 1352.

The **kite** is brought to Europe from China, where it has been known for many years.

1316 **Spectacles** improve the vision of old people who are becoming long-sighted. The short-sighted have to wait until 1450 for the invention of suitable lenses.

1320 The Chinese invent **playing cards.**

1346 The English use **cannon** for the first time against the French at the battle of Crécy. The idea comes from the Arabs who themselves had borrowed it from the Chinese.

The first **locks** are fitted with vertical sluice-gates. Ninety years later, Leonardo da Vinci invents the modern lock-gate.

1396

1389   Monarchs and noblemen have their **commodes** upholstered in rich materials. In the 17th century the palace of Versailles will contain 274 'business chairs'.

1450   The silvered **looking-glass.**

Carriages with leather-spring suspension.

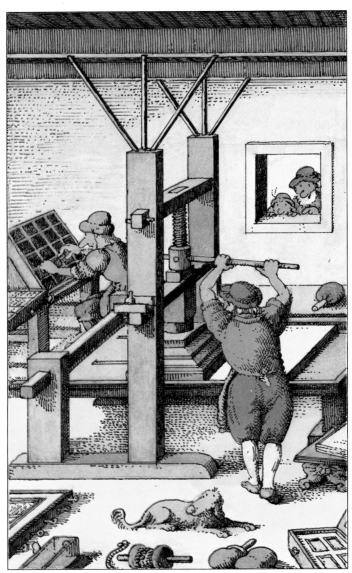

The Chinese are said to have invented **printing** around AD 800.

A Dutchman, Laurent Coster, is the first European to think of carving each letter of the alphabet separately in wood. In 1423, he prints an eight-page book, containing letters of the alphabet and some Sunday prayers. Coster is not, however, destined to become famous.

Some years later, Gutenberg perfects the process by casting the letters of the alphabet in molten lead. He also invents the printing press and uses it in 1448 to print his famous '42-line' Gutenberg Bible in Mainz.

King Louis XI of France introduces the **postal service,** and mail coaches now travel the length and breadth of the kingdom. In Britain mail coaches are introduced 300 years later. Before this, the mail is carried by mounted post-boys.

12 October 1492

Christopher Columbus lands in the West Indies, hitherto undiscovered lands. Fifteen years later, a geographer mistakenly attributes the discovery to Amerigo Vespucci and calls the New World America.

1490 **China plates** and **napkins;** people (rich people) no longer have to wipe their mouths on the tablecloth.

1492 Christopher Columbus discovers **cocoa** in America. He also finds **pineapples, tobacco** and the **turkey.**

1534 Pizarro's men return from Peru with **potatoes** but it will be many years before they become popular in Europe.

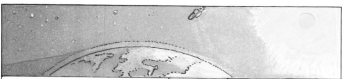

The Earth moves and travels round the sun! So says the astronomer Copernicus although many refuse to believe him…

1543

1554 **Arithmetical symbols.**

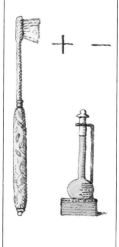

Anatomy. William Harvey will discover the circulation of the blood in 1628.

1570 The Spanish ambassador to France introduces the **toothbrush**.

1592 Using a principle known to the Ancient Greeks, that heated air expands, Galileo perfects the **thermometer**.

The first **screw** is a threaded nail which is screwed in but cannot be removed until the arrival of the screwdriver 100 years later.

1608 Galileo also invents the **telescope** and proves Copernicus right. But few people believe him.

Around 1560

The **glazier.** Technical progress means new jobs!

The **sedan chair.**

The folding **fan** made of lace or feathers.

1600   Switzerland has the first **national anthem.** *God Save the Queen* (or *King*) will be composed in 1740, and the *Marseillaise* in 1792.

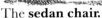

1607   Monteverdi writes *Orfeo*, the first opera, in **staff notation.**

1610   The Dutchman Cornelius van Drebbel invents the **microscope. Tennis** (and rackets). When the player serves, he shouts **'tenez!'** ('here you are!' in French); the name sticks.

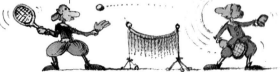

1625   The first form of **public transport** appears in London. It is a large carriage with windows and anyone can travel in it for the price of a few pennies. Not surprisingly, the **umbrella** is an English invention.

The French statesman Richelieu makes the use of the round-ended **table knife** compulsory, perhaps to discourage assassins at the meal table.

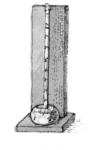

1642   The French philosopher and mathematician Blaise Pascal designs a **calculator.** 1644: Torricelli's **barometer** indicates what weather to expect.

1653
An early form of **snakes and ladders** comes from Venice.

Paris has the first **letter-box**.

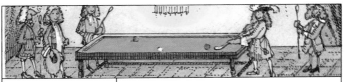

1666   Doctors advise King Louis XIV of France to play **billiards** for the sake of his digestion and he makes the game fashionable. It had appeared in Britain in the 16th century.

1658   In Sweden the Bank of Stockholm issues the first **banknote**.

1668   Dom Pérignon, a Benedictine monk in charge of a vineyard belonging to a monastery in France, invents **champagne.**

By thoroughly cooking tough meat and even bones, the pressure cooker provides cheap food for the poor.

1670   The Dutchman Christiaan Huyghens invents the **watch** fitted with a spiral spring.

1681   Frenchman Denis Papin designs the **pressure cooker**.

The **café** comes to Paris, having made its appearance in Mecca, Venice and London. The first Parisian café still exists today.

1684

Sorbets are made with snow or ice kept cold in straw and placed in cool cellars. The Chinese had known the recipe for many years.

The **screwdriver,** at last, and therefore modern screws.

Wallpaper, imported from China, becomes highly fashionable in London.

Corkscrews and **corks,** which replace wax for sealing bottles.

1690   In Italy Antonio Stradivari creates the finest and best-known of violins — the **Stradivarius**.

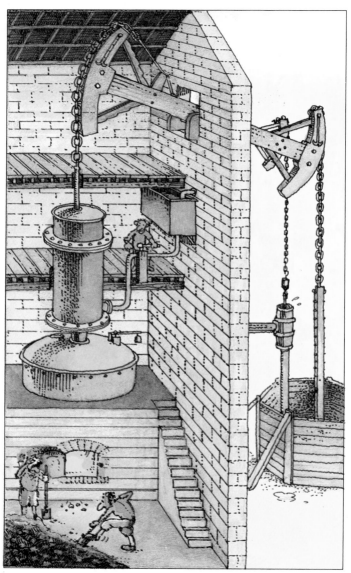

Rails and wagons are used in England to carry coal out of the mines. They have already been in use in Transylvanian mines for 200 years. They are the first **railways.**

The steam engine. In ancient times, Hero of Alexandria invented his 'aeolipyle', the ancestor of the modern jet engine. In France, Denis Papin designs a steam engine which, through lack of funds, is never actually built. In constructing his pressure cooker, however, he invents the safety valve, an essential component of steam-powered equipment.

In 1712, the Englishman Thomas Newcomen builds the first modern steam engine. Its rocking beam is used to pump water out of a coal mine.

In 1765, Scotsman James Watt increases the machine's efficiency by perfecting various components such as the rotary movement.

By the end of the 18th century, more than 80 steam engines are in use in England, driving rolling mills, steam hammers, looms, threshing machines and flour mills.

Thanks to the coal-burning blast furnace invented in 1707, all sorts of objects, from cooking-pots to machine parts, are made in **cast iron.**

18th century

Around 1707

Travelling showmen delight village audiences with their **magic lantern** picture shows.

1711 George Frederick Handel's trumpeter, John Shore, invents the **tuning fork**. It still keeps musicians in tune today.

1726 William Chambers produces the first **encyclopaedia;** 30 years later, Dr Johnson will publish his famous dictionary.

Braces.

The **rubber eraser**.

1728 The first game of **cricket** is played between Kent and Surrey.

Benjamin Franklin notices that sharp metal objects attract lightning, and designs a **lightning conductor**. He also invents a new kind of **wood-burning stove** and even a **rocking-chair** for sitting in front of it.

1755   In France, Boudin builds the first **kitchen stove**.

1759   The **silhouette** takes its name from Etienne de Silhouette, Chancellor of the French Exchequer. He has to retire early and cuts out silhouettes as a pastime.

1762   King Louis XV of France passes a law making it compulsory for all actresses and female dancers to wear **knickers.**

1764   **Spinning jenny.** The mechanical spinning machine.

1765 In Paris Monsieur Boulanger opens the first **restaurant**. His sheeps' trotters in white sauce are an instant success.

1762 The Earl of **Sandwich** is so fond of gambling that he has snacks of bread and meat brought to him, instead of stopping the game for a meal.

1769 Cugnot's **steam lorry** has front-wheel drive and is the first automobile.

1770 **Baths** made of sheet metal.

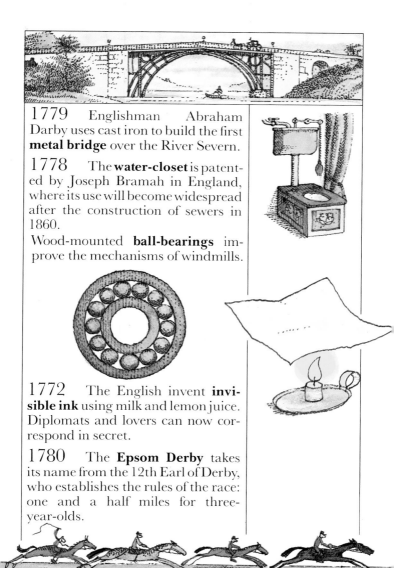

1779 Englishman Abraham Darby uses cast iron to build the first **metal bridge** over the River Severn.

1778 The **water-closet** is patented by Joseph Bramah in England, where its use will become widespread after the construction of sewers in 1860.

Wood-mounted **ball-bearings** improve the mechanisms of windmills.

1772 The English invent **invisible ink** using milk and lemon juice. Diplomats and lovers can now correspond in secret.

1780 The **Epsom Derby** takes its name from the 12th Earl of Derby, who establishes the rules of the race: one and a half miles for three-year-olds.

1782

Fire insurance started in England after the Great Fire of 1666. Over 100 years later the idea is introduced to France by Etienne Delessert.

1783 The French Montgolfier brothers invent the **hot-air balloon**. Its first passengers are a cock, a sheep and a duck.

1785 The first **air disaster** comes when François Pilâtre de Rozier dies in his blazing hot-air balloon attempting to cross the Channel.

1 January 1788 The first issue of **The Times**.

Three natives of Chamonix **climb Mont Blanc** in the Alps, the highest mountain in Western Europe. The first woman will climb it in 1808.

1788   The **diving-suit.** Now people can explore under the sea.

In America John Greenwood transforms his mother's spinning wheel into a terrifying **dentist's drill**.

1790   **Camembert cheese** from Normandy in France.

False teeth are made of hippopotamus ivory. George Washington, who became President of the United States in 1789, has a set.

1790 Count de Sivrac's **celerifer** has no pedals or handlebars, but at least it has two wheels, just like its descendant, the bicycle.

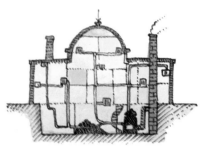

1792 **Central heating** is installed in the Bank of England in London.

Cigarettes are hand-rolled. The first machine-made cigarettes will be produced in Cuba in 1853.

7 April 1795 **The metric system**. Adopted in all western countries, except Britain, Ireland, Canada and the United States.

Claude Chappe's visual **telegraph** or semaphore is faster than a horse! The signals are placed at intervals of about 15 kilometres, and in clear weather a message takes a mere 20 minutes to cover 1000 kilometres.

1794

In 1837 British inventors will replace these visual signals with electric signals.

1795 Enclosed in wood, the **pencil** is invented by the Frenchman Conté to take the place of the English graphite stick.

1797 Jacques Garnerin **parachutes** out of a hot-air balloon above Paris.

Vaccination against smallpox by Dr Edward Jenner.

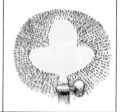

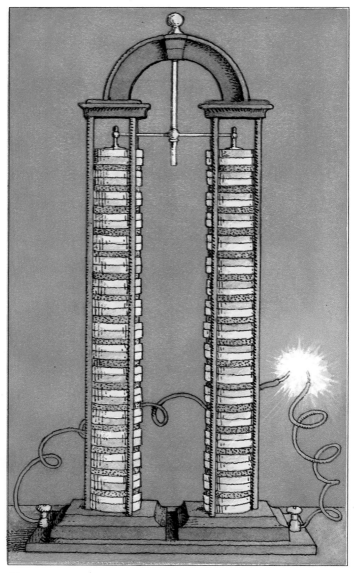

In 1807, Napoleon makes **driving on the right** obligatory throughout Europe.

Why? Perhaps just to be different from the English, who have always used the left-hand side of the road. This makes it easier for a driver to draw his sword on meeting an enemy or to shake hands on meeting a friend.

The electric battery. The Greeks and Romans knew of the existence of electricity but could do no more than obtain a few sparks by rubbing amber or sulphur.

In 1800 an Italian physicist called Alexandro Volta discovers that contact between two metals can produce electricity. He builds columns of alternating zinc and copper discs, isolating each pair with felt. Continuous electric power is generated between the two poles of this battery. For the first time an electric 'current' can be put to practical use.

Napoleon also devises a civil code, the *Code Napoléon*, which will serve as a basis for much of France's future civil law.

Beginning of the 19th century

1805 **House numbers** in Paris. Streets lying parallel to the River Seine have numbers running in the same direction as the river flows.

1801 **The Jacquard loom** can automatically weave patterns into cloth or carpets.

1803 American Robert Fulton takes his **steamboat** *Clermont* up the Seine, but receives no encouragement from the French government. Napoleon sees little future in steam.

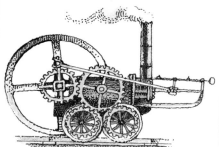

1804 In South Wales, Richard Trevithick's **steam locomotive** is used instead of horses to pull wagons in coal-mines.

The *Elise* makes the first **steam crossing of the Channel**. Three years later, the *Savannah* will travel to America, although with the help of sails as well as steam.

1816

1805 French doctor Laënnec invents the **stethoscope**: cough please!

1807 We can thank Bertel Sanders in Denmark for the **push-button**.

1817 Baron Drais invents the **draisine**. The earlier celerifer now has handlebars, but still lacks pedals.

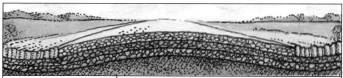

1815

What we call 'tar macadam' is made of asphalt and will be used to make roads for many years.

Scotsman John L. MacAdam discovers a method of paving roads in such a way as to make them extremely resistant to wear.

1818 Dr James Blundel performs the first **blood transfusion** at Guy's Hospital in London. An attempt to give a person sheep's blood 150 years earlier had failed.

The Aztecs had known about rubber's waterproof qualities for a long time.

1821 Erard's **piano,** in Paris. It is the first grand piano as we know it today.

1824 The first man to make a **raincoat** is a Scot, MacIntosh.

The Society for the Protection of Animals is founded in London, where you can already be fined for beating your dog.

Matches are invented in England.

1826 The English invent the **tin can.** It is less fragile than the glass preserving jars designed in 1809 to store food for Napoleon's soldiers. Since the tin opener is not yet invented, you have to use a hammer and chisel.

Photography. Joseph Nicéphore Niepce manages to record an image using his pin-hole box. Unfortunately, the subject has to pose for eight hours! In 1839, Jacques Daguerre will reduce the time to 30 minutes.

In England, Fox Talbot produces a 'negative', from which he is able to print as many 'positives' as he wishes.

1824

Sea bathing becomes fashionable in the summer of 1822 thanks to the Duchess of Berry, the daring granddaughter of King Charles X of France. Of course, the new railways will make it easy to get to the seaside.

The railway. Wagons running along iron rails are already in use in coal-mines, and in 1804 the first steam engine with wheels appeared. All that is needed is to put the two together and this is done on 27 September 1825 on a 50-kilometre stretch between Stockton and Darlington in England.

Five years later, in 1830, the first major railway carrying steam locomotives opens between Manchester and Liverpool, complete with a tunnel over two kilometres long. Every country in the world adopts its 1.44 metre gauge except Spain and Russia, which are perhaps afraid of invasion by train. Railway construction will lead to the development of many other industries, including the building of embankments, tunnels, viaducts, stations, depots and all sorts of workshops.

The **steel pen-nib** comes from Sheffield and replaces the quill pen used until then.

Middle
of the
19th
century

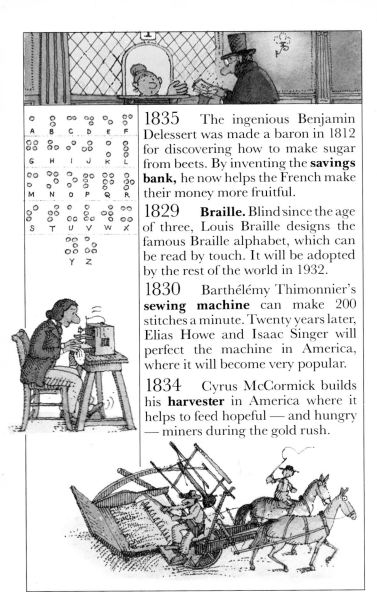

1835 The ingenious Benjamin Delessert was made a baron in 1812 for discovering how to make sugar from beets. By inventing the **savings bank,** he now helps the French make their money more fruitful.

1829 **Braille.** Blind since the age of three, Louis Braille designs the famous Braille alphabet, which can be read by touch. It will be adopted by the rest of the world in 1932.

1830 Barthélémy Thimonnier's **sewing machine** can make 200 stitches a minute. Twenty years later, Elias Howe and Isaac Singer will perfect the machine in America, where it will become very popular.

1834 Cyrus McCormick builds his **harvester** in America where it helps to feed hopeful — and hungry — miners during the gold rush.

Sir Francis Pettit Smith launches the **screw**-driven *Archimedes*. Seven years later, a steamship fitted with screws will easily outrace a paddle-steamer.

The **lawnmower** is invented in Great Britain. It is pulled by a horse which wears rubber boots over its hooves to avoid damaging the lawn.

1838

Poker. Very popular with cowboys in the Wild West.

1836 American Samuel Colt invents the **revolver.**

1839 **Stick no bills!** From now on English advertisers can reserve wall space and it is forbidden to stick up posters at random.

5 July 1841   Thomas Cook organises travel for 500 members of a temperance society. The **travel agency** is born.

1840   The first **postage stamp**, the Penny Black. Great Britain, as the birthplace of this invention, does not have to put its name on its stamps.

A .—   N —.
B —...   O ———
C —.—.   P .——.
D —..   Q ——.—
E .   R .—.
F ..—.   S ...
G ——.   T —
H ....   U ..—
I ..   V ...—
J .———   W .——
K —.—   X —..—
L .—..   Y —.——
M ——   Z ——..

The Morse Code

24 May 1844   The first **tele-graph message** is transmitted between Washington and Baltimore by an American painter, Samuel Morse, who converts the alphabet into a series of dots and dashes. The message is the quotation: 'What hath God wrought?'

1846   Boston doctors William Morton and John W. Jackson use ether as the first **anaesthetic.** Thirty years later, the first local anaesthetic will be administered by a young Austrian: Sigmund Freud.

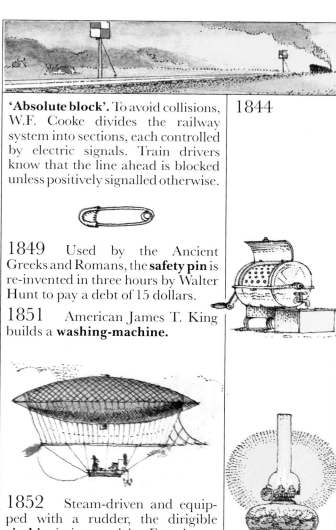

'Absolute block'. To avoid collisions, W.F. Cooke divides the railway system into sections, each controlled by electric signals. Train drivers know that the line ahead is blocked unless positively signalled otherwise.

1844

1849 Used by the Ancient Greeks and Romans, the **safety pin** is re-invented in three hours by Walter Hunt to pay a debt of 15 dollars.

1851 American James T. King builds a **washing-machine.**

1852 Steam-driven and equipped with a rudder, the dirigible **airship** is invented by Frenchman Henri Giffard.

1852 The **oil lamp** with mantle.

1856   **The 'General'.** The driver and engineer of this famous wood-burning locomotive had as much trouble from buffalo on the track as from outlaws and Red Indians.

1853   The **lift.** Elisha Otis demonstrates in New York the first fast and safe lift. Until the invention of his safety system, people were afraid to use passenger lifts in case the rope snapped.

Every flat soon has one of Lebon's patent **gas cookers**.

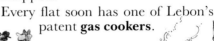

1856   **Aniline ink** and chemical dyes.

1859   The first modern **derrick** goes up in Pennsylvania. The owner, Colonel Drake, discovers oil at 21.

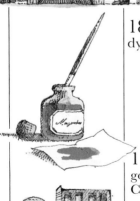

1860   The American L. Yale invents the **combination lock.**

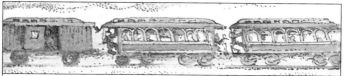

George Mortimer Pullman's **sleeping cars** have lavatories, wood panelling and carpets. Twelve years later, Pullman will invent the dining car as well.

1860 Louis Pasteur's **pasteurization** process sterilizes milk and will soon be used on other foods.

The **tin-opener** is invented in America, 40 years after the tin, probably by soldiers of the Civil War.

1862 The **ice rink** in New York's Central Park.

1858 The first great **ocean-going liner**, the *Great Eastern*, is built by Isambard Kingdom Brunel. Over 200 metres long, she can carry 3,000 passengers — but only 35 people book cabins for her maiden voyage.

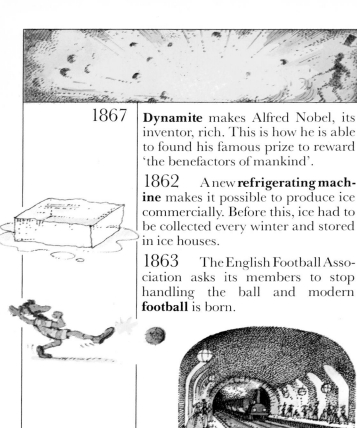

1867 **Dynamite** makes Alfred Nobel, its inventor, rich. This is how he is able to found his famous prize to reward 'the benefactors of mankind'.

1862 A new **refrigerating machine** makes it possible to produce ice commercially. Before this, ice had to be collected every winter and stored in ice houses.

1863 The English Football Association asks its members to stop handling the ball and modern **football** is born.

January 1863 The first underground railway — **the Tube** — opens in London. In its first year of service, this steam-powered system transports nine-and-a-half million people.

1865 The **penny-farthing** and, finally, pedals, thanks to the French firm of Michaux & Son.

The Salvation Army is founded in London; its soldiers defend the faith, fight against poverty and play music in the street.

1878

1869   Frenchman Louis Ducos successfully prints the first **colour photograph.** In 1904 the Lumière brothers will set up the first colour-photography business.

1870   Belgian Gramme's **dynamo** generates electricity in an uninterrupted direct current, which can then be brought to houses and factories.

1876   Alexander Graham Bell patents his **telephone** just two hours before rival inventor Elisha Grey tries to do the same. 'Ahoy, ahoy, Watson. Are you there?' are the first words spoken over a telephone line.

The invention of the **transformer** in 1883 allows **high-tension wire** to carry electricity 14 kilometres from an alpine waterfall to the city of Grenoble in France.

The electric light bulb. Since the invention of the battery, scientists have been searching for a filament that would glow. The most methodical of these is the American inventor Thomas Edison, who tries everything he can think of, silk thread, charred paper, bamboo, human hair . . .

On 21 October 1879 a length of cotton thread taken from his wife's sewing basket glows for 45 hours — electric light is born! Edison will soon produce his bulbs in quantity.

In 1877 Thomas Edison finally manages, after many years, to reproduce sound artificially on his 'talking machine', the **phonograph.** The first words engraved in wax are 'Mary had a little lamb'.

1878   Writer Robert Louis Stevenson designs a **sleeping bag** to keep him warm while travelling with his donkey in the Cevennes mountains in France. The bag is made of thick waterproof canvas lined with sheep's wool.

1874   Philo Remington's **typewriters** are produced in munitions factories, shut down since the end of the American Civil War.

1878   Augustin Mouchot's **solar water-heater** drives a printing-press linked to a steam engine.

1879   The **cash register** is invented in the USA. In 1892, William Buroughs will make one that can print receipts.

1880   In London, Mr J. Walters unveils his elegant three-wheeled **roller skates**, although the type we use today had been patented 17 years earlier by New Yorker James Plympton.

1881   **Electric trams,** sparks and all, appear on the streets of Berlin. Invented by Werner von Siemens.

1880   **Chewing-gum.** American inventor Thomas Adams bases it on an ancient Mayan recipe.

1883   Nine storeys high and with brick walls and a metal frame, the first **skyscraper** is built in Chicago by William LeBaron Jenney.

1884   The impeccably dressed French civil servant Eugene Poubelle makes 'household residue receptacles' obligatory. The French call them *'poubelles'*, we call them **'dustbins'.**

The first **fountain pen.**

1887   Daimler builds the first petrol-driven **motor car.** But he will soon have competition from Karl Benz, Panhard and Levassor, de Dion and Bouton, the Peugeot brothers, Henry Ford, Louis Renault …

The **Eiffel Tower** is designed and built in two years by French engineer Gustave Eiffel. The focal point of the Paris International Exhibition, it is made of 15,000 pieces of iron, is 320.75 metres high and weighs 9.700 tonnes.

1888 **The bicycle.** Already equipped with a chain, a saddle and identical wheels, the old velocipede now has pneumatic tyres, thanks to a Scottish vet, J. Dunlop.

1889 **Photography for everyone:** 'Press the button and we'll do the rest.' Eastman invents the film roll and a simple camera, the Kodak Box Brownie.

1890 The McLeod American Pneumatic Company of New York installs **air conditioning** to circulate warm air in winter and cool air in summer.

9 October 1890 **Powered flight.** In Paris Clement Ader rises a few centimetres above the ground in his steam-powered *Éole*.

1891 **The electric iron.**

The **electric fan:** yet another new invention using Gramme's dynamo generator.

1891 The 'noble art' of **boxing** adopts the Marquess of Queensberry's rules. The sport practised by Greeks and Romans had been re-invented in the 18th century.

Jean Rey and Jules Carpentier invent the **periscope.** Submarines can now see without being seen.

1892 **Coca Cola.** Atlanta chemist Dr Pemberton's famous recipe contains 15 ingredients, including the still-secret '7X'.

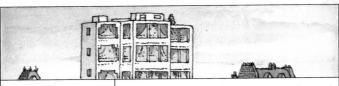

Reinforced concrete strengthened with iron rods is invented in Paris by François Hennebique.

1893 Designed by American W.L. Judson, the **zip fastener** owes its name to the advertising slogan 'Zip, it's open, zip, it's closed!'

Aspirin. German chemist Adolph von Bayer fixes in tablet form extract of willow, whose properties were known to the Ancient Greeks.

1894 Alphonse Bertillon of the Paris police uses **fingerprints** to identify criminals.

1895 The Werner brothers choose the name **motorcycle** for their engine-powered bicycle.

Radiography. Wilhelm Roentgen discovers the existence of mysterious rays which allow him to photograph the inside of his wife's hand: X-rays, of course.

The **first automobile race** takes place between Paris and Rouen with 15 competitors. The Marquis de Dion's steam tractor is the fastest, recording an average of 22.2 kilometres an hour.

22 July 1894

1895   In Wisconsin, USA, King Camp Gillette thinks up the **safety razor** with disposable blades.

28 December 1895   In the lounge of the Grand Café, Boulevard des Capucines, Paris, Auguste and Louis Lumière unveil their invention: the **cinema.**

| 8 April 1896 | Baron Pierre de Coubertin is the father of the modern **Olympic Games.** He revives them after a 1,500-year interval. |

1895 The French Michelin brothers invent the removable **tyre** for motor cars.

2 June 1896 **Radio.** Russian Alexander Popov transmits a 'wireless' message over a distance of 250 metres. Three years later, Marconi will broadcast across the English Channel.

1897 Toasted **corn-flakes** are invented in a Michigan woodcutter's cabin by the Kellogg brothers as a means of feeding their fourteen little brothers and sisters.

1900   The first line of the Paris **Metro** is inaugurated on 19 July. Each station has beautiful art nouveau decorations.

1898   Louis Renault designs the **gearbox** complete with gear-lever and reverse.

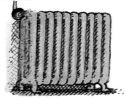

1899   The central heating **radiator.**

1 May 1899   In Paris the Belgian driver Jenatzy does **100 kilometres an hour** in his electric car.

The ***Jamais-Contente*** (the *'Never Satisfied'*).

The **Tour de France** bicycle race begins on 1 July 1903. It is contested in six stages over a distance of 2,428 kilometres. Sixty cyclists set off but only 22 complete the course. It will continue to be an annual and increasingly popular event.

20th century

On a cold and windy morning in December 1903, Orville Wright rises three metres above the ground and flies for about 30 metres — a 12-second miracle!

He and his brother Wilbur built their **aeroplane** and its motor in the workshop where they usually make bicycles.

Until now, the majority of attempts at flight have been made in machines with wings that flapped like a bird's. But, thanks to their observation of birds gliding, the Wright brothers have been able to perfect a method of keeping their machine in the air after take-off.

Leo Hendrik Baekeland, a Belgian living in the USA, invents Bakelite. This first 'thermoformed' **plastic** is tough and resistant.

1907 The *Mauritania* ushers in the era of the great **transatlantic liners.** For 22 years, this floating palace will make the fastest crossings from Southampton to New York, covering the distance in four days, 16 hours.

1905 Einstein is 26 when he publishes his famous **theory of relativity.**

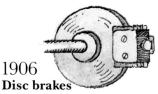

1906
Disc brakes

are the brain-child of car designer Alexandre Darracq.

1905 Winsor McCay's **strip cartoon** 'Little Nemo' begins appearing daily in the *New York Herald*.

1907 Lord Baden-Powell has the idea of **scouting** as a way of providing physical and moral education for boys.

1906 American de Forest's **triode lamp** gives wireless a voice; until now it has been limited to morse, but the triode enables it to transmit speech and music through sound waves.

3D photography projected on to a special screen.

In Chicago **instant coffee**, invented by Japanese Satori Kato, is first sold to the public.

1908 The **Rolls Royce Silver Ghost**. According to the advert, 'the greatest car in the world'.

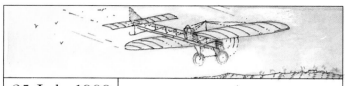

25 July 1909

At 4.40 in the morning, Frenchman Louis Blériot leaves Calais and **flies over the Channel** to Dover.

1908

James M. Spangler's portable electric **vacuum cleaner.**

It is more practical than Cecil Booth's 1901 vacuum lorry, which cleaned houses from the street by means of a long tube.

1909   To produce his famous **Model T Ford**, Henry Ford also invents the **production line**.

1913   The *New York World* gives its readers the first **crossword puzzle** on 21 December.

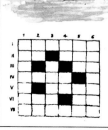

During the First World War the British use 60 **tanks** in the Battle of the Somme. The French follow suit with tanks built by Renault.

1916

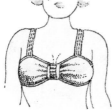

1914   The **brassière** is designed by American heiress Caresse Crosby, who has clearly inherited her inventive streak from her grandfather, Robert Fulton, inventor of the steamship.

1914   Red and green **traffic lights** appear in Cleveland, Ohio. Amber will come later, in New York.

1918   The first **supermarket** is opened in the USA by Kroger Grocer & Baking Co., a big grocery chain.

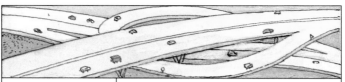

1924   The first real **motorway** links Milan and Varese in Italy.

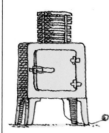

1920   The **wristwatch.** An idea taken over from First World War soldiers who used to attach their pocket watches to their cuffs.

1922   The domestic **refrigerator** appears in America. It will reach Europe five years later.

1924   **Paper tissues**

The radio-set. There are already six-and-a-half million wireless receivers in the world.

26 October 1926   Al Jolson in *The Jazz Singer* — the first **talking picture.**

20 May 1927 Alone in his *Spirit of St Louis*, 25-year-old Charles Lindbergh makes the first non-stop **flight across the Atlantic**, landing near Paris after 33 hours 30 minutes in the air.

1928 The **aerosol spray.**

Adhesive tape.

1929 Ruined by the Wall Street Crash, American Charles Darrow invents **Monopoly.**

1930 Oscar Barnack invents the **Leica camera** in which 36 small-format negatives can be taken on cine-film.

Frozen foods are sold commercially by Clarence Birdseye, who had hit on the idea of fast-freezing fresh foods 10 years earlier while hunting in Labrador.

1933   Streets, cinemas and shops are making use of **neon lighting**, invented by Georges Claude in 1910.

1930   Many American houses now have their own automatic **washing machines.**

1931   Blind people throughout the world adopt the idea, pioneered in Paris, of carrying a **white stick.**

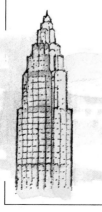

1931   American Colonel Jacob Schick makes and patents the **electric razor.**

1932   The **Empire State Building:** 102 floors, 6,400 windows and 448 metres high.

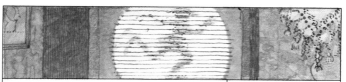

On 22 November the BBC begins a series of regular **television programmes** thanks to the invention of television by Scotsman John Logie Baird.

1932 **Kodachrome**: Violinist Leopold Godowsky and pianist Leopold Mannes discover a process that makes colour photography accessible to everyone.

1935 In Hollywood *Becky Sharp* is the first film made **in Technicolor** using the method developed by Herbert T. Kalmus.

1936 The German government asks Ferdinand Porsche to design a 'Volkswagen', 'car for the people' in German. Over 20 million **'Beetles'** will be produced.

1936

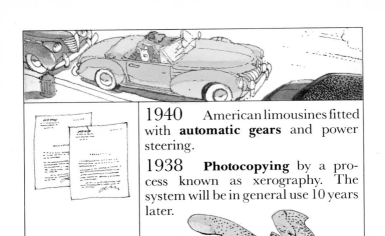

1940 American limousines fitted with **automatic gears** and power steering.

1938 **Photocopying** by a process known as xerography. The system will be in general use 10 years later.

1938 **Nylon**, invented by the French firm Du Pont de Nemours. Its appearance in the form of ladies' stockings coincides with the arrival in Europe of US soldiers in 1944 . . .

1939 **DDT** is invented in Switzerland and used by the US Army against fleas and mosquitoes.

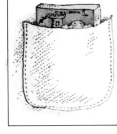

Igor Sikorsky fits a vertical helix to the end of his **helicopter**; this small detail makes his machine stable and safe.

New York publishers Simon & Schuster launch the pocket-format **paperback**.

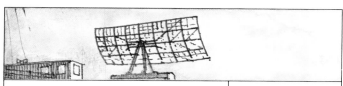

To provide early warning of enemy air-raids, Britain protects itself with a system of 'Radio Detection and Ranging', better known as **radar.**

1940

The Biro brothers patent the **ballpoint pen**, which is first sold in Argentina. Milton Reynolds' model will be produced in 1945.

Tape recorders are sold for the first time in Germany, although Valdemar Poulsen discovered the principle in 1898.

1941 **Penicillin** is successfully tested on a patient. It had been discovered in 1928 by Scottish doctor Alexander Fleming.

1942 **Nuclear power.** Enrico Fermi masters chain reaction in Chicago and sets up a nuclear reactor.

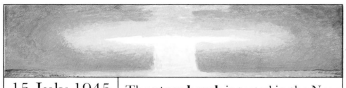

| 15 July 1945 | The **atom bomb** is tested in the New Mexican desert. On 6 August 1945 at 7.30 in the morning it will be dropped on the Japanese city of Hiroshima, killing 39,000 of its inhabitants. |

1944 The Messerschmitt ME 262 **jet** is brought into service by the German Airforce. It is the beginning of the end for the 'turboprop' plane.

1946 The Eniac **electronic computer** can multiply together two 10-figure numbers in three-thousandths of a second. It weighs 30 tonnes and uses 18,000 valves.

1947 **Instant photographic prints** become possible when Edwin Land markets his Polaroid camera.

The first **medical transplant** takes place in Boston, USA, when Dr Joseph Murray and his team succeed in grafting a new kidney. In 1967 South African surgeon Christiaan Barnard performs a heart transplant, but the patient dies 10 days later.

1954

14 October 1947   The American aeroplane Bell X-1 breaks the **sound barrier** at 1078 k.p.h.

1947   **Contact lenses.**

1948   The **micro-wave oven** is a peaceable spin-off from radar technology.

1949   The **long-playing** 33 or 45 rpm record replaces the old 78 which had only 8 minutes playing time in all.

The Citroën '2cv'. Still going strong today.

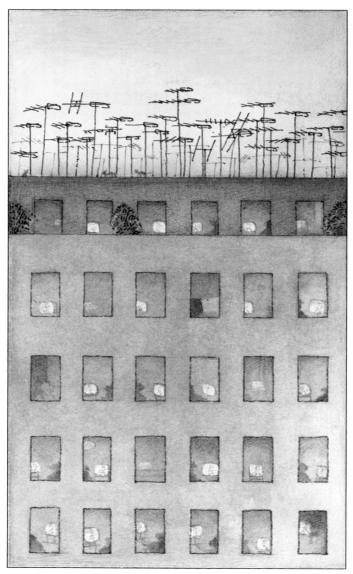

84

Cinemascope. Invented some years earlier in France by Henri Chrétien, the wide-screen process or 'cinemascope' becomes Hollywood's main weapon in the fight against TV.

Television. Using some of the principles that were later to be applied to television, 'wire-photos' were being transmitted between London and Paris as early as 1907. After years of experimenting, John Logie Baird had developed a form of television by 1926. Twelve years later the Russian-born American inventor Vladimir Zworkyn perfected the first practical television camera, the iconoscope. Only then was television ready to become a household item.

However, it was the live transmission in 1953 of Queen Elizabeth II's coronation — the first great televised spectacular — that persuaded thousands to invest in a set.

The **scooter** first becomes popular in the fifties. It is ideal for zipping around in traffic, and is still a favourite in sunny climates.

With the American invention in 1948 of the **transistor**, portable radios become possible. The electronics industry has never looked back.

1950s
to
1980s

| 29 May 1953 | Sir Edmund Hillary and Sherpa Tensing climb 8,848 metres to **the top of Mount Everest** in Nepal. |

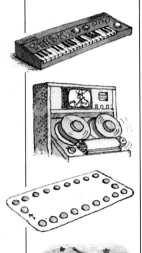

1953   On 5 October, at the University of Columbia in the USA, Chopin's Polonaise in A flat, opus 53, is the first piece to be played in public on a **musical synthesizer.**

1956   Inventor Alexander M. Poniatoff added 'ex' for excellence to his initials and called his **magnetic video recorder** 'Ampex'.

The **contraceptive pill** by Harvard University's Dr Pincus.

4 October 1957   The USSR launches *Sputnik*, the first **man-made satellite.** Four years later, a dog, 10 mice and several insects have made the journey. Yuri Gagarin will become the first man in space.

1958   High-fidelity **stereo** on record.

1960 'Light Activation by Stimulated Emission of Radiation' — **Laser.**

Asahi Pentax and the Japanese photo industry begin their conquest of the world with the **reflex camera.**

1958 A Pan Am Boeing 707 **airliner** begins regular service between New York and Europe.

11 June 1959 Christopher Cockerell's **hovercraft** crosses the Channel 50 years after Blériot.

1963 The Dutch firm Philips invents the **minicassette** and the portable cassette recorder.

London fashion designer Mary Quant presents the **mini-skirt.**

16 July 1969 **Men on the moon.**
Neil Armstrong, Edwin Aldrin and Michael Collins fly there in Apollo 11.

Thanks to live **colour television** millions of people can watch Armstrong and Aldrin walking on the moon.

Jumbo-jets and charter flights put palm-trees closer to our reach.

1971 The **microprocessor** —
the 'miracle chip' — is the power behind pocket calculators, giant computers, video games and industrial machinery.

1972 **Hang-gliding** becomes a
popular, if dangerous, sport.

25 July 1978 The first
test-tube baby, Louise Brown, is born in England.

1979   In Japan, Akio Morita of Sony invents the **walkman** so as to play golf while listening to music... without disturbing other players!

Videocassettes arrive from Japan.

The first user-friendly personal computer, the **Apple II**. Its young inventors, Steve Jobs and Stephen Wozniak of San Francisco, built their original machines in a garage.

1980   **Bar codes** for labelling goods are invented in North America.

1980   The **Nuclear Magnetic Resonance** body scanning machine.

The **removable self-stick note** is invented by chemical engineer Arthur Fry, to mark the pages in his hymn-book at choir practice on Sundays.

14 April 1981 The **space-shuttle** *Columbia* glides in from its first space-voyage, having travelled at 25 times the speed of sound.

With the **auto-focus camera**, taking pictures is simple, and the **mini-lab** will develop your snaps in about an hour.

Laser **compact discs** start to replace LP records.

1984 The **camcorder** brings a whole new dimension to home-movies.

1986 **Minoxidil** is the first cure for baldness. Used at the Washington Hospital Centre in the United States to cure hypertension, it is found to have an unexpected side-effect: it causes hair growth.

1987 **Four-wheel-drive** gives greater stability at corners and improves steering during manoeuvres.

The **facsimile machine** or **fax** uses the telephone system to send images and texts instantaneously to other faxes anywhere in the world.

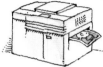

1988 The **colour laser photo-copier** is another development in laser technology.

Colourisation modernises old black-and-white films by colouring them.

The **cellular** or **cordless phone**, originated by the Swedes, is now to be seen everywhere, in homes and cars.

A professor at the University of Ohio in the United States produces a recipe for **ice-cream for pets.** It is a great success amongst discerning canines.

1990 **This book.**

Index of inventions and inventors

94

The inventor of this book

Jean-Louis Besson was born in 1932, the year the Empire State Building was constructed.

Not long after, he was at nursery when the BBC launched television.

He was an altar boy swinging incense while the Swiss were inventing DDT.

A bare two months before the first successful atomic reactor, he entered the Lycée Voltaire in Paris. It was there that he worked out and perfected his technique of doodling on exercise books, a skill which stood him in good stead when he was later employed in an advertising agency.

A year after the invention of the mini-skirt, he decided to become an illustrator. Since then he has worked on magazines, cartoons, films, books and posters.

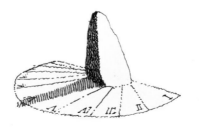